I0485720

Drawing

Drawing for Beginners

Drawing

Drawing for Beginners

© Copyright 2015 Michael Adams

This document is geared towards providing exact and reliable information in regards to the topic and issue covered. The publication is sold with the idea that the publisher is not required to render accounting, officially permitted, or otherwise, qualified services. If advice is necessary, legal or professional, a practiced individual in the profession should be ordered.

- From a Declaration of Principles which was accepted and approved equally by a Committee of the American Bar Association and a Committee of Publishers and Associations.

Table of Contents

Introduction

A lot of people think that only people born with the skills can really draw well. Though it is true that, drawing comes naturally to innately creative people, it is not something that cannot be achieved by learning. All you need is motivation that you can do it and a helping hand (or in this case, a helping book) to guide you in the right direction.

In this book we will teach you the basics or fundamentals on how to draw. We will study the proper proportions, stages and right angles to get the proper pose, and adding details based on your desired subject. This book will also teach you the human face and hands which are the tricky parts.

Once you've completed your figure, the final parts of this book will show you the stages of the drawing in summary. This may all seem too much to handle, especially to first timers, but with a little time and effort, you will surely get the hang of it.

Thank you for downloading this book. Happy Reading!

Chapter 1 - The Basics Of Drawing (Tools)

Like any other facets or factors in life, one need to know the basics on a certain subject or task at hand – and learning to draw is no way different from that. Ever wondered how Picasso produced such wonderful paintings? How about the magnificent painting of Michael Angelo on the ceiling of the Sistene Chapel? No pressure there! But of course you don't need to be expert in just a snap of a finger. Drawing takes a lot of time to develop but as long as you have the passion and patience to keep on pursuing this dream, then there won't be any problems.

The purpose of this book is to help you understand and start your passion to draw. You may not have an innate talent for drawing, but acquiring the knowledge and putting it into practice plus enthusiasm and determination will definitely develop your targeted skill.

Since the day you were able to hold a pencil, you are already starting to draw but those scribbles did not have any meaning to you at all. You just want to doodle and be fascinated with the colors and shape that the pencil produce on the paper. But as time goes by, your interpretation of these drawings mature and from careless scribbles, you are now more aware of using some dots, lines or shapes. The more you are exposed to the environment, the more you get to know about the different strokes, curves and dimensions; it becomes complicated which blinds you to be artistic. And this might be another reason why you are having a hard time to draw. No need to worry as we are going to let your inner artistry out in the open.

Now, before we begin with the step by step guidelines on how to draw you need to know that basic tools in order to start drawing. I have listed some of the things you need to get started:

Pencil. As a first timer, you will have to deal with a lot of erasures in your attempt to draw figures. Sure, nowadays, there are pens out in the market for drawing and some manufacturers are producing ink erasers but I've got to tell you this, ink erasers are not erasers per se. Typically they just masticate your paper until the ink is gone and believe me, you'll notice that your paper becomes thinner to the point where if you'll draw on the exact spot and erase it again, your paper will be torn. So stick with the use of a pencil. No.2 pencil is popular as it is the regular pencil we use since our toddler years. It is not that hard and not that black. You see, pencils are graded based on the hardness and the blackness of the lead used. So as a beginner, use the No.2 pencil first and when you progress, get yourself a 4B or a 5B pencil.

Eraser. Of course, everybody makes mistakes and in order to correct your drawing, you need a trusty eraser to help you correct them. There are different types of eraser you could find at a local craft or book store but pick a rubber one. You might want to consider the size of the eraser as well.

Working Area. Look for a working area which you are most comfortable with. It must be with the proper lighting so if it gets dark when you draw, you'll be able to see it clearly. Design your desk the way you want it and think of how it will inspire you to sit down and practice what you'll learn from this book.

Ruler. An ordinary 12-inch ruler is fine as you'll not use it that much.

Paper. You can use standard bond paper for your artwork or if I were to recommend a better alternative, purchase a sketchbook. The purpose of the sketchbook is it will be your collection of drawings and it can serve as a record of your progress.

Wait! I know you are excited to start the process but it is also essential to know the basic elements of a drawing. This shall be quick. Below are the basic elements to ponder:

Line. Everyone will agree that line is the basic form or element of any type of drawing. But did you know that in reality or what we call the real world, line does not exist? Because it is considered as two-dimensional (the height and the width). If we incorporate line in our drawing, line separate two areas from each other but in reality it is a surface of a plane. Another example is in the 2D world, we call four lines connected on all ends, a square but in a 3D world, we call it a cube.

Shape. There are no further explanations for this as shape is always presented by connecting or linking 2 or more lines. It is basically formed by lines.

Proportion. Proportion is the measurement of your subject and for our topic, the body figure. It dictates the average or standard size of the parts of the body figure such as lower limbs are longer than your upper limbs or a female torso is thinner than a male one.

Perspective. It is the figment of your imagination or simply the illusion which make distant objects look smaller while closer objects look bigger.

Shadow. Creating a shadow in your drawing will add a realistic feature on it.

Chapter 2 - The Basics Of Drawing (Hand Positions)

Aside from the tools and other information, one important element in creating your drawing is learning the different hand positions. Hand position will depend greatly from different factors, such as the requirement of your drawing, be it for detailing or for shading, also on the way your paper rests, whether it lays flat or angle steeply. At first it will not be easy to adapt to the different hand positions. Most likely, your hand is already comfortable with the standard way of holding a pencil when drawing, same way your hold a pen when writing. This won't be a problem, most artist hold the pencil the same way the hold a pen. But by drawing in the same hand position all throughout your drawings will limit you to the same mark that that position makes on your drawing. Variety is a very important part of any artwork, and in drawing, the best way to create variety is to learn the different types of hand positions to make a variety of marks on your drawing helping it achieve depth. Now let us see the different type of hand positions and their applications.

Standard Position

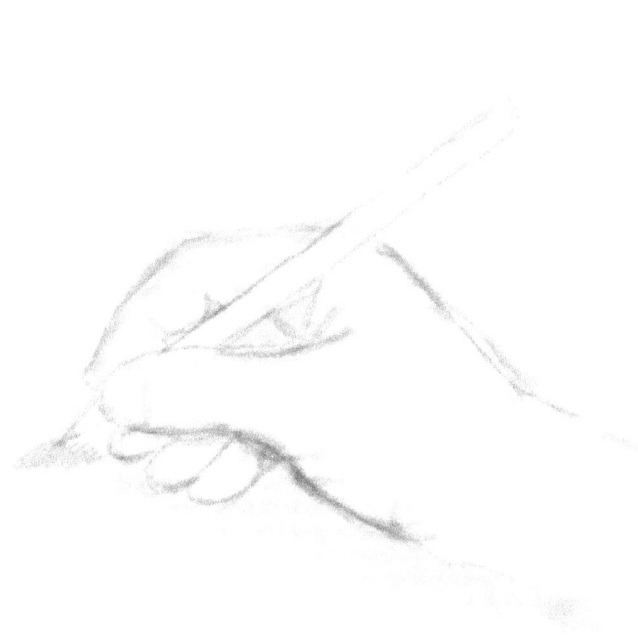

This is the most natural way of holding the pencil. This is how we hold any writing material when we started learning to write. This will probably be your go-to position whenever you start drawing. This position gives you a lot of control over your pencil strokes. This is what you will use for initial sketches and minor detailing. Most people only draw in this hand position, but as mention above, this will limit the variety you can apply to your drawings.

Drumstick Position

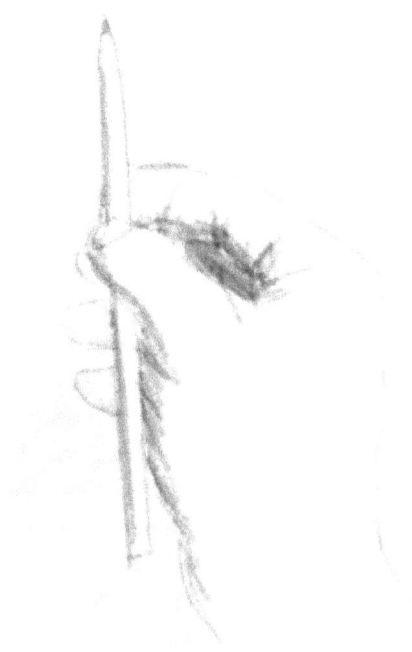

In this position, you will hold the pencil with the index finger and the thumb, using the other fingers for stability. Don't hold the pencil too tightly as this will minimize the freedom your pencil to create a variety of marks. This position is commonly used for adding details with shading and a variety of strokes. When drawing in a large scale, this position is also widely used.

Paint Brush Position

In this position the pencil is held like a paint brush by holding it upright and letting the back end rest on the crest between the index finger and the thumb. This position is most commonly used for creating light marks

Heavy tip Position

In this position, use our middle finger and thumb to hold the pencil then with your index finger, apply pressure to the tip of the pencil. This will help you achieve heavy and wide marks on your drawing helping you create depth and when filling large areas with heavy shade.

Braced Position

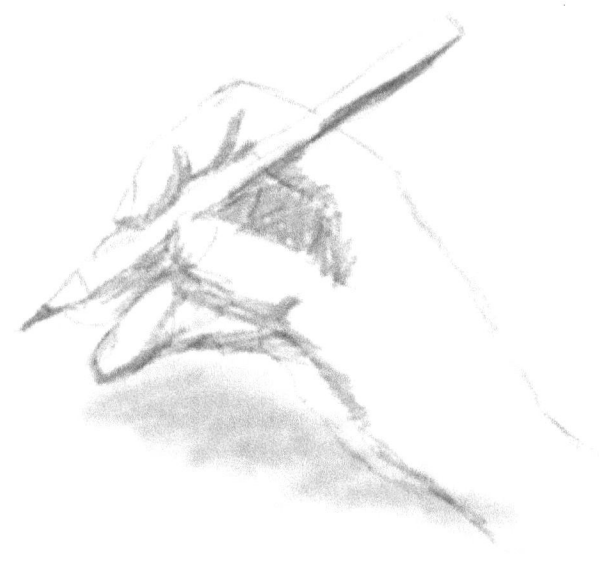

In this last position, the pencil is held very much the same as the first one, Standard Position. The difference is, the pencil is held upright and more pressure is applied to the tip. This position is used for defining outlines and adding fine details to your drawing. This is usually used for finishing touches.

Chapter 3 - Toning And Shading

In this chapter, we will tackle some useful tips of toning and shading which will help to improve your drawing skills.

These drawing techniques enlivens a certain artwork, it brings life and dimensions to the drawing. The simple lines you draw on paper come to life by using toning and shading. It is like a 3-Dimensional effect straight to your paper, wherein it emphasizes the body and angles of your masterpiece.

Toning

Toning is a technique used in drawing for creating / adding depth to your artwork. This is achieved by using highlights and shadows, and in drawing, the best way to get this is by applying shades. The following are the techniques used for applying shades on your drawings.

Uses of toning

Toning is very important in the field of drawing, it may be a bit tiring to do… but this technique makes a big difference when applied.

Below are the different usages of toning in drawing:

- It is mainly used to accentuate the plain areas of a drawing
- It brings different proportions to your artwork
- It forms focal pointers of interest
- It creates an optical illusion
- It brings depth to the certain areas of a subject matter

Useful tips of toning

Tone drawing may be a bit tiresome to do, but there are useful tips to make tone drawing much easier. Here are some ways:

Pen and brush quick toning

- Draw the outlines using water-soluble ink pen, such as a fountain pen or fine liner pen.
- Then use a thin paint brush and dip into clear water, create some strokes that you want to tone.

One color quick toning

- Pick a color on your palette that will produce different gradients.
- Brush the lightest parts of the drawing with a thin wash of the color.
- Next is the moderate tone color, brush the medium colored areas of your drawing.
- Mix the dark tone, which is the final tone (more paint less water.) Brush the dark colored areas.
- Tip: Farthest distance should be pale dark, middle distance is medium dark tone, and the nearest should be the darkest.

Chalk and charcoal toning

This useful toning tip is perfect to picture the lights and darks of a drawing.

- Use a brown paper or packaging paper for this useful tip, the brown paper serves as the medium tone.
- Grab a white chalk and charcoal, the white color serves as the light tone while the charcoal as the dark tone.

Blending

Sample Blending

This technique is achieved by scribbling on the part of your drawing where you want to add shading and using your fingers, or pretty much any material, to blend the graphite to get a smoother outcome. You can use any material like cloth, tissue paper or even cotton buds to get different kinds of textures.

Circulism

This is done by drawing small circles over each other slowly building the tone that you want to achieve. This is best when trying to get realistic shading for the skin

Dark Shades

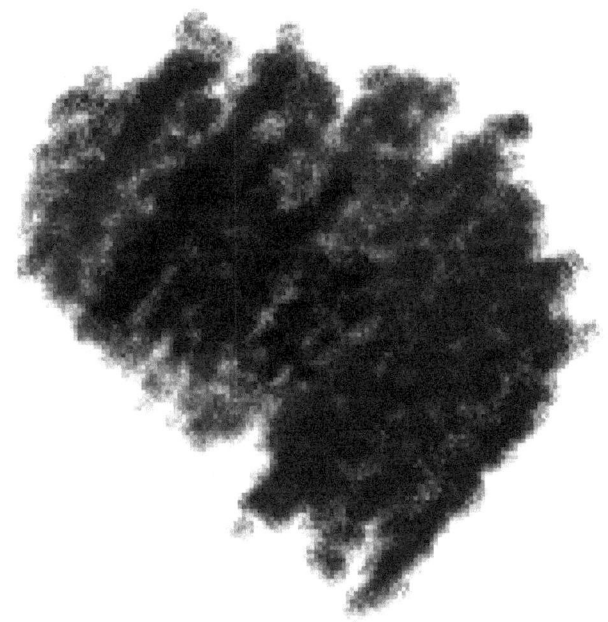

This technique is pretty much the same as the same as the first two but giving it a bit more pressure to get the dark shade necessary for gaps and what not.

Cross Hatching

Loose Cross Hatch

Tight Cross Hatch

This is achieved by drawing lines the overlap each other. This gives your drawings a more artistic look. This technique can also be done in two ways, tight cross hatching and loose cross hatching. Use lose for light shades and tight for darker ones

Uses of shading

Shading might be simple to look at, but it contributes so much to the 3D effect of a certain drawing.

Below are the different usages of shading:

- It accentuates distance
- It serves as the shadowy depth of a drawing
- It illustrates different kinds of levels in one drawing
- It makes the drawing more realistic

Useful tips of shading

There are different types of shading; these can be utilized as useful tips for you to put shadings in your artwork.

Below are the useful tips of shading:

Density variation

Draw the lines very near or far apart from each other for line shading.

Pressure variation

Pressure refers to the lightest to darkest of shades. The darker the shade, the harder the pressure for the drawing.

Use various grades of pencils and hues of color pencils

This is the very useful tip, use different grades of pencils hues of color pencils for easy shading.

Chapter 4 - Portrait Drawing

By definition, portrait drawing is the art of illustrating a person when the prominent feature is the face, most notably the expression. This is the reason the most portraits don't look candid. Subjects are more often than not composed.

Step 1

In your canvas, create an oval roughly in the center, make sure it is not too big that other elements of your drawing will not fit your paper nor is it too small that there will be too much blank space when you're done.

Step 2

Draw a vertical line at the center of your oval. This will be your guide on the symmetry of the both sides of the face. But if the head is not facing front, your line should be place off center. If your subject's head is facing even a little bit to the left, your line should be on the left side of your ovals center. And if it's even slightly facing to the right, your line should be to the right of the center.

Step 3

Draw a horizontal line in the center of your oval overlapping the vertical line you just drew, making a cross. This will be your guide for the eyes. But again, take note of the head of your subject. This line should not always be at dead center. If your subject's head is tilted backward, this line should be above the center, and alternately, if the head is tilted forward, the line should be blow the center.

Step 4

Roughly below the middle of the eye line and the "chin," draw another horizontal line, this will be your lip line. Roughly below the middle of that and the eye line, again draw another horizontal line, this will be your nose line.

Step 5

Now that you have your basic guidelines for the face, you can start drawing the outline of your subject, no need to be too polished at this stage. Just draw a rough outline of the hair, eyes, nose, lips, etc.

Step 6

When you're satisfied with your outline, start adding the details, personally, I like starting with the hair because it mostly overlaps everything on the face.

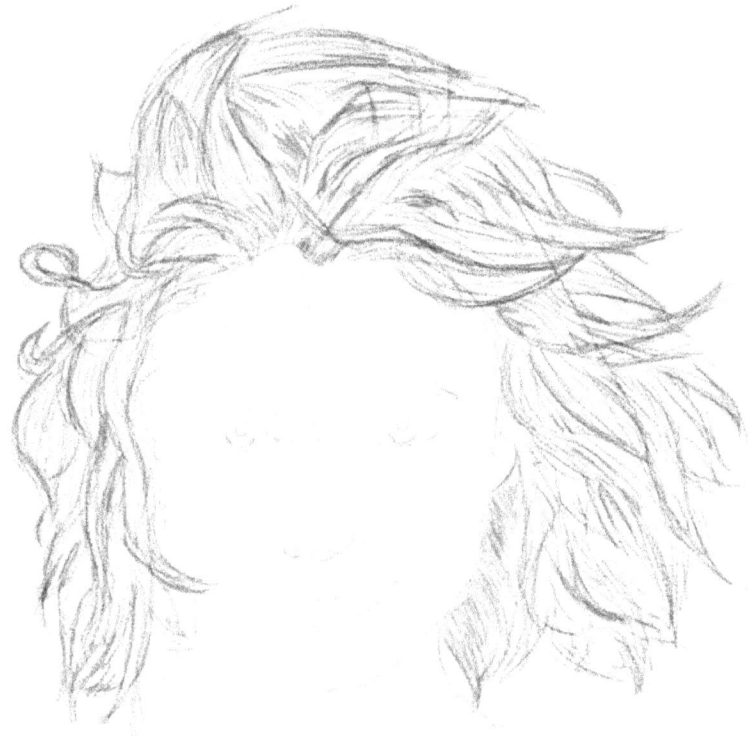

Step 7

When you're done with the hair, you can start detailing the eyes, nose and lips

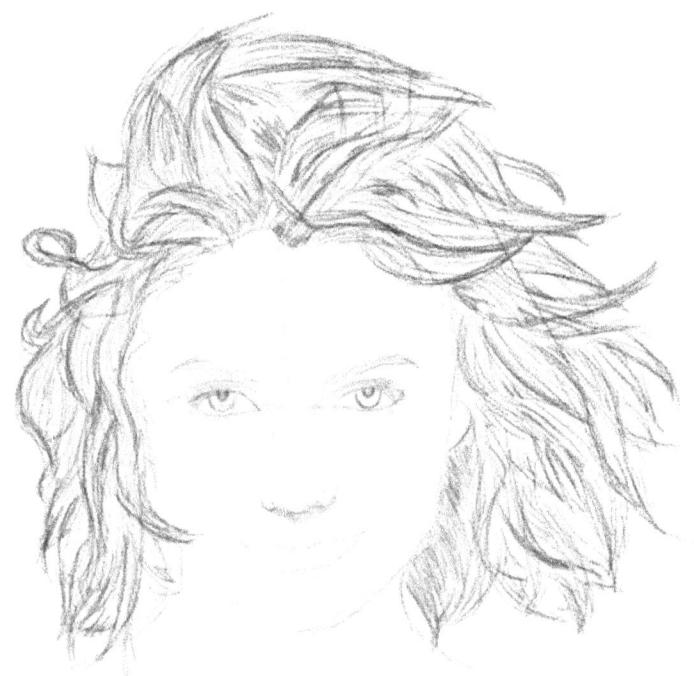

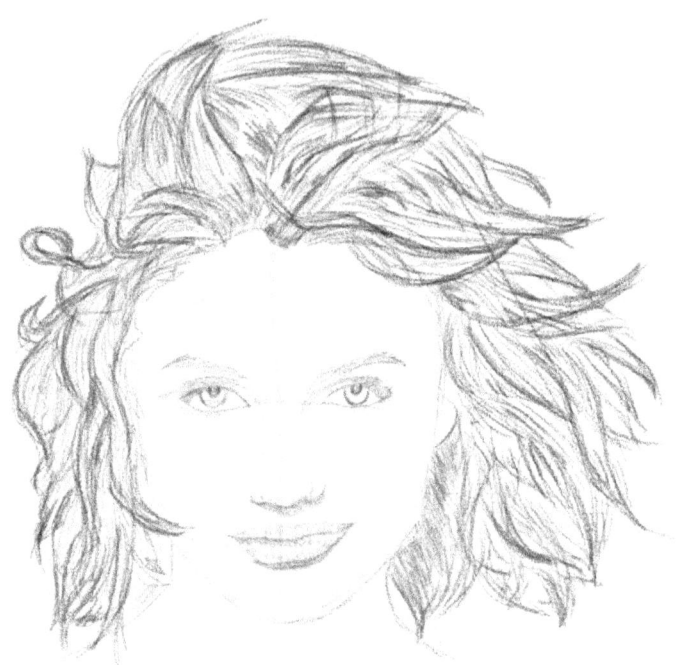

Step 8

Just continue adding details using the hand positions and toning techniques mentioned on the previous chapters. Add shadows and darken outlines to create depth.

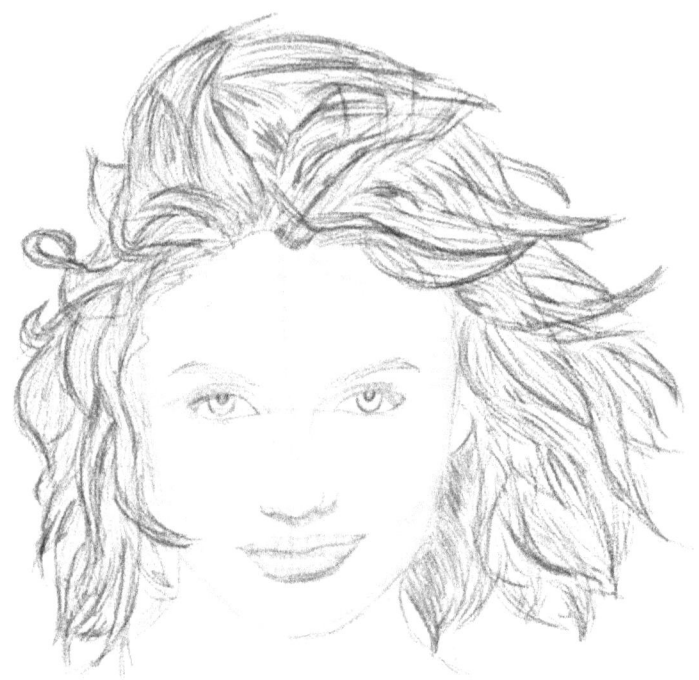

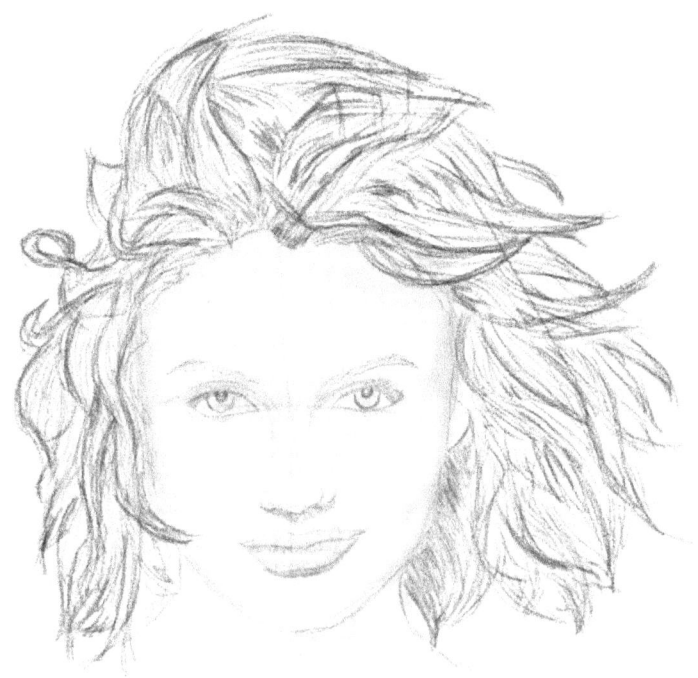

Step 9

For the finishing touches, what you can do is add a bit of highlight. I'm sure you're asking how to do that considering we're only using a pencil. What I do is, I lightly shade the area around the part I want to add the highlight then using my eraser, I slightly "draw" the highlight parts. Some artists call this the reverse drawing technique, by erasing parts of the graphite you can create highlights, another way of doing this is by again shading around the area of the highlight, but this time completely avoiding it.

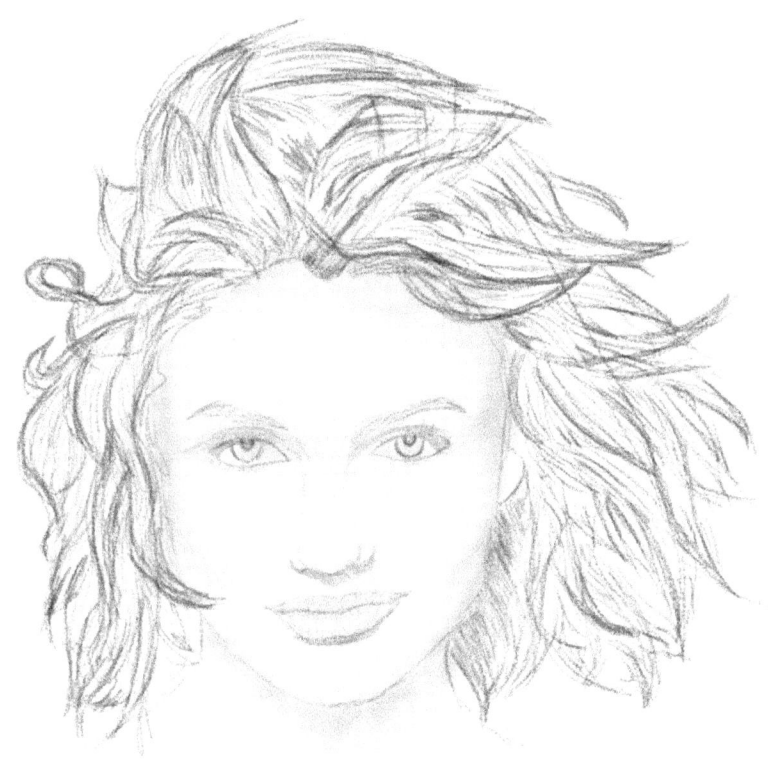

Drawing the human face and its expressions have been around for centuries and was mostly reserved for the wealthy and the nobility in the olden times. Nowadays, this popular form of art is still very much alive and evolving. As a beginner, here are some useful tips to start you with portrait drawing. Here's a few more useful information to create a portrait drawing:

Ready your materials

When starting out, you need not buy expensive art supplies first. You only need to buy the basics which are the following (arranged according to importance):

- Paper or Drawing Pad
- Pencil set
- Eraser
- Blending stump
- Ruler
- Sharpener

Of course quality usually comes with a price so better stick to the known brands like Faber Castell and Pentel. You can also start off with an A3 or A4 sized paper or drawing pad with a paper weight of 200 g/m². Choose between an ordinary rubber eraser and putty rubber.

It is also best to work on a room with enough light, preferably daylight, and a hard solid surface.

Start with the specifics

Learn to draw the different features of the face first, one at a time. Try to perfect the details of the eyes, nose, lips, and ears and practice drawing the variations of each feature, like thin and thick lips, small and big eyes, or narrow and broad nose. You can practice with photographs or a live model.

How to draw the Eyes

Step 1

Drawing the eyes is like just any other drawing, you start with drawing a simple outline.

Step 2

Shade the pupil and make sure to make it a dark.

Step 3

Shape the iris. For better effect, draw lines starting from the pupil going out to the edge of the iris.

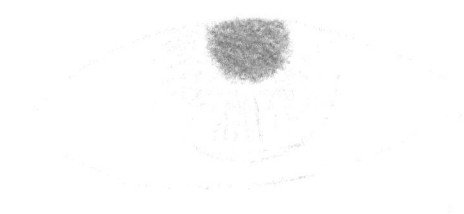

Step 4

Start drawing in the lashes. Draw small lines from the out line of the eyes goin out. For better effect, flick your pencil at the end.

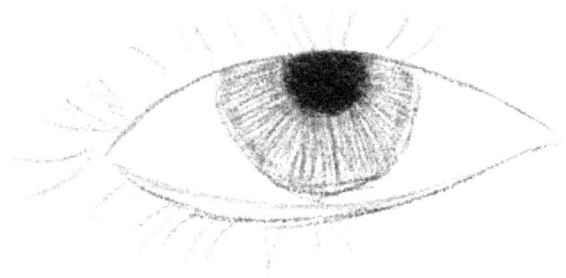

Step 5

Darken the outline of the eye and highlight the pupil and iris.

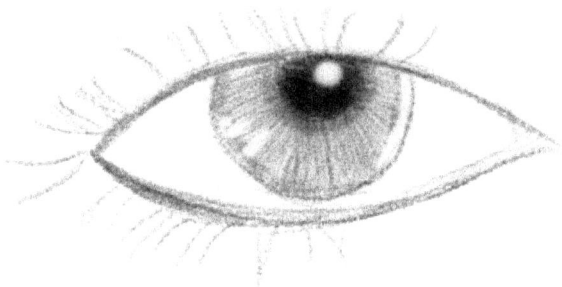

Step 6

Draw the eye brows, this will help you determine where to add shadows.

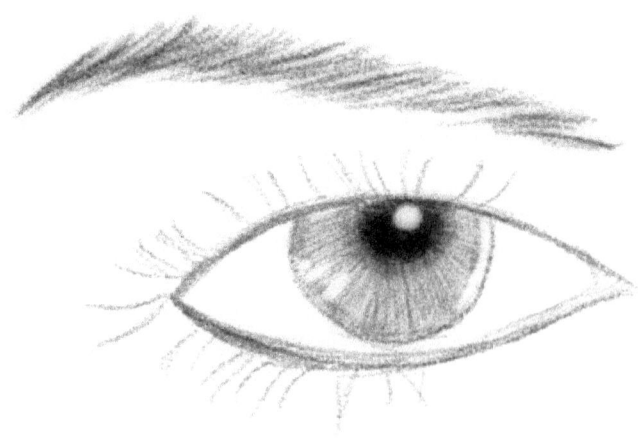

Step 7

Add shadows.

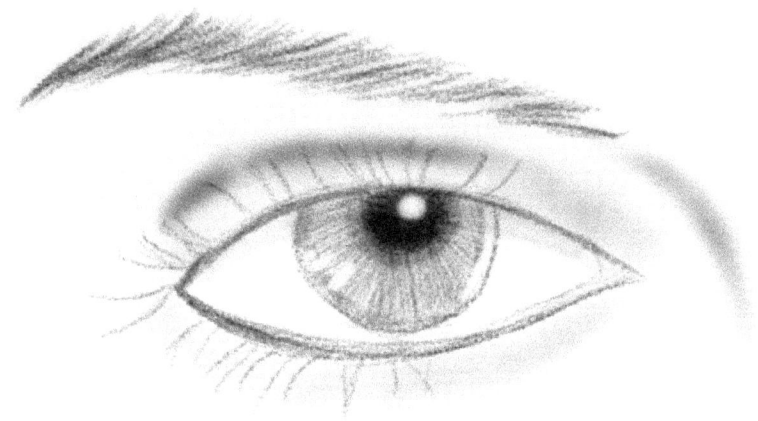

Step 8

To get more realism, add more toning and fine details

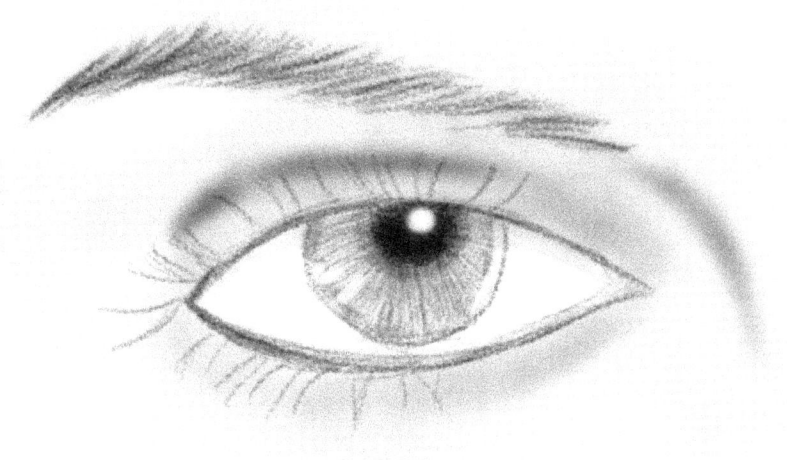

How to draw a Nose

Step 1

Again we start by drawing a rough outline, but this time around, make it a bit more on the lighter side. When drawing the nose, the less solid lines, the better.

Step 2

Drawing the nose is mostly done by toning, shadows and highlights. Start with the lightest shadow. Scribble and smudge a light shade onto your paper. If your outline gets smudged as well, just redraw it lightly

Step 3

To add the highlights, use an eraser. Just erase the parts where you think the highlights should be.

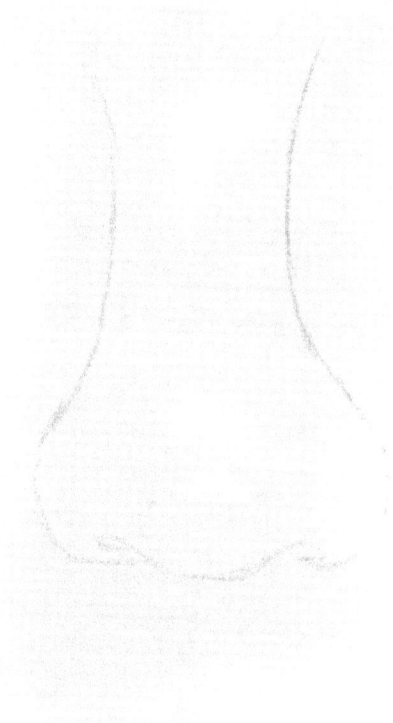

Step 4

You can add another layer if you think your drawing needs
more depth or to add a darker shade.

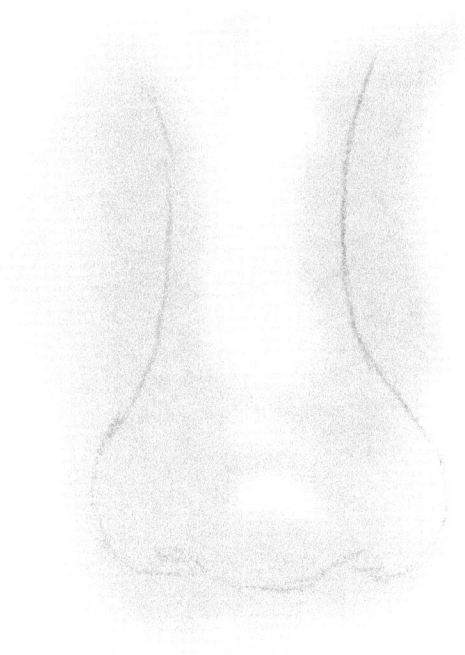

Step 5

When adding shades, make use of lines that follow the contour of the nose, before you smudge them.

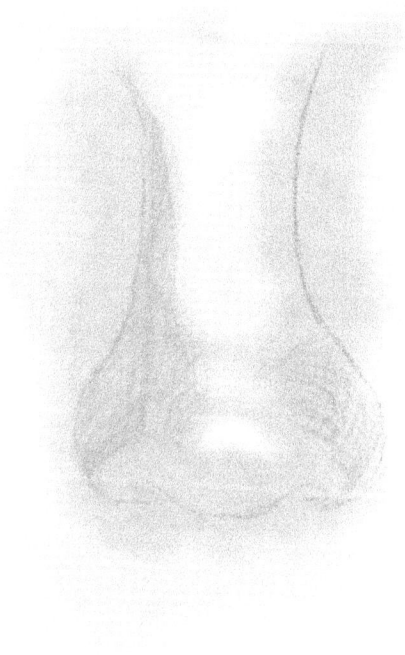

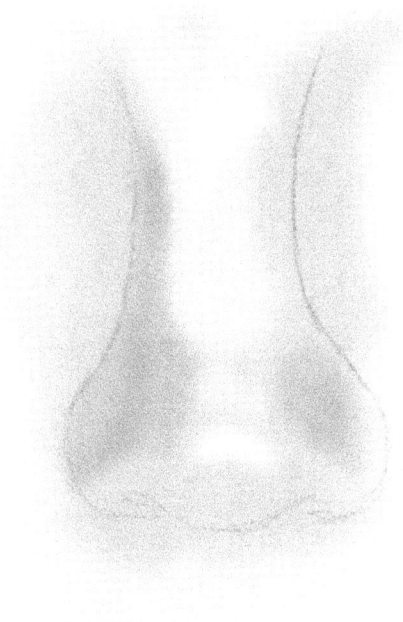

Step 6

Add some finishing touches to give it some depth.

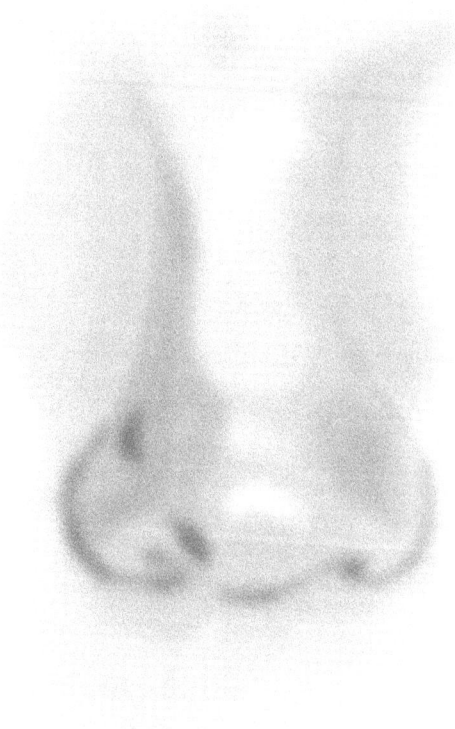

How to draw the Ears

Step 1

As per usual, we start by drawing the rough outline.

Step 2

Add more details with solid lines. Unlike the other parts of the face, the ears have more outlines as details.

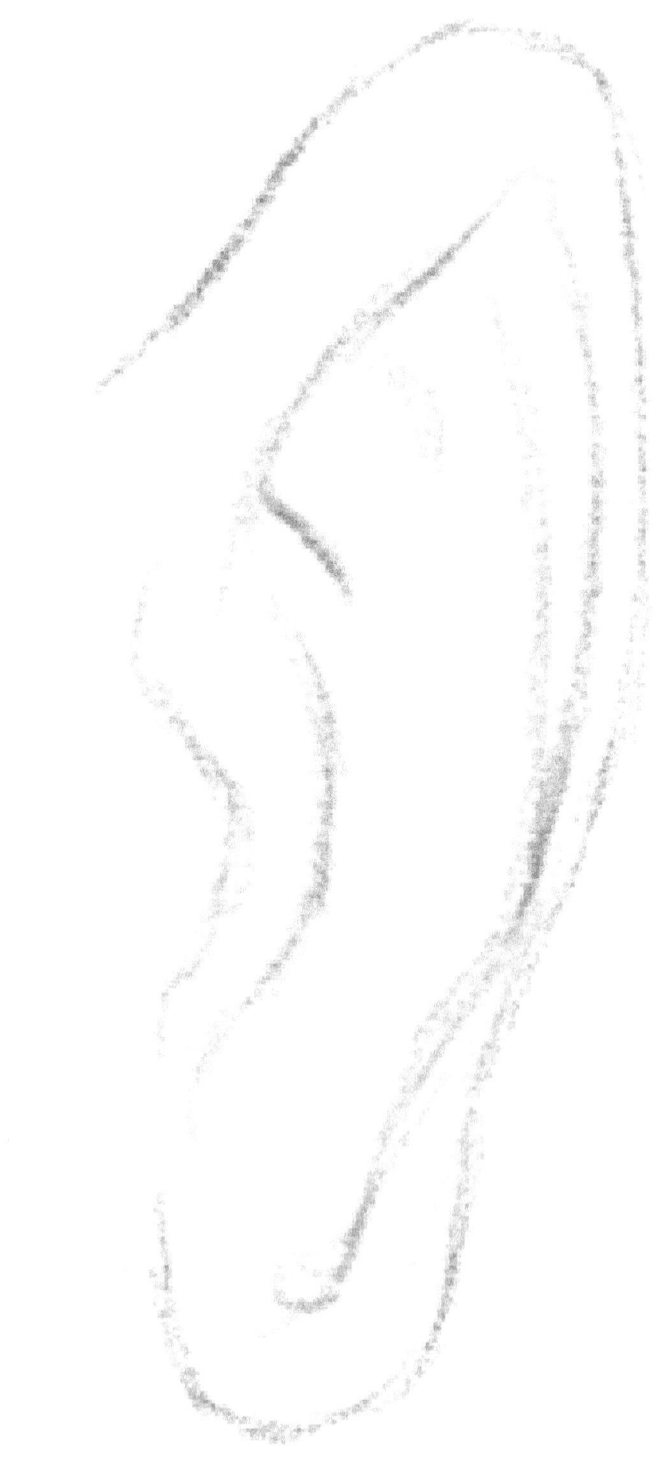

Step 3

Start Adding the shadows.

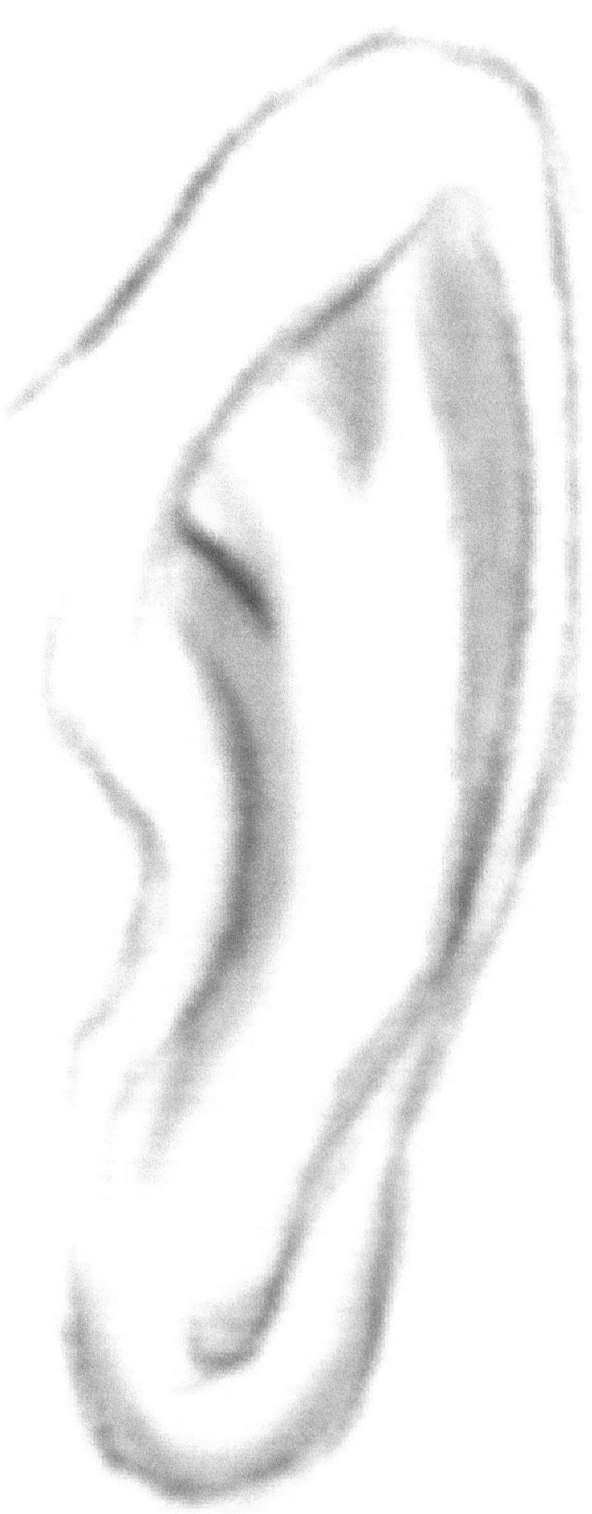

Step 4

Share the whole drawing lightly end use an eraser to create the highlights.

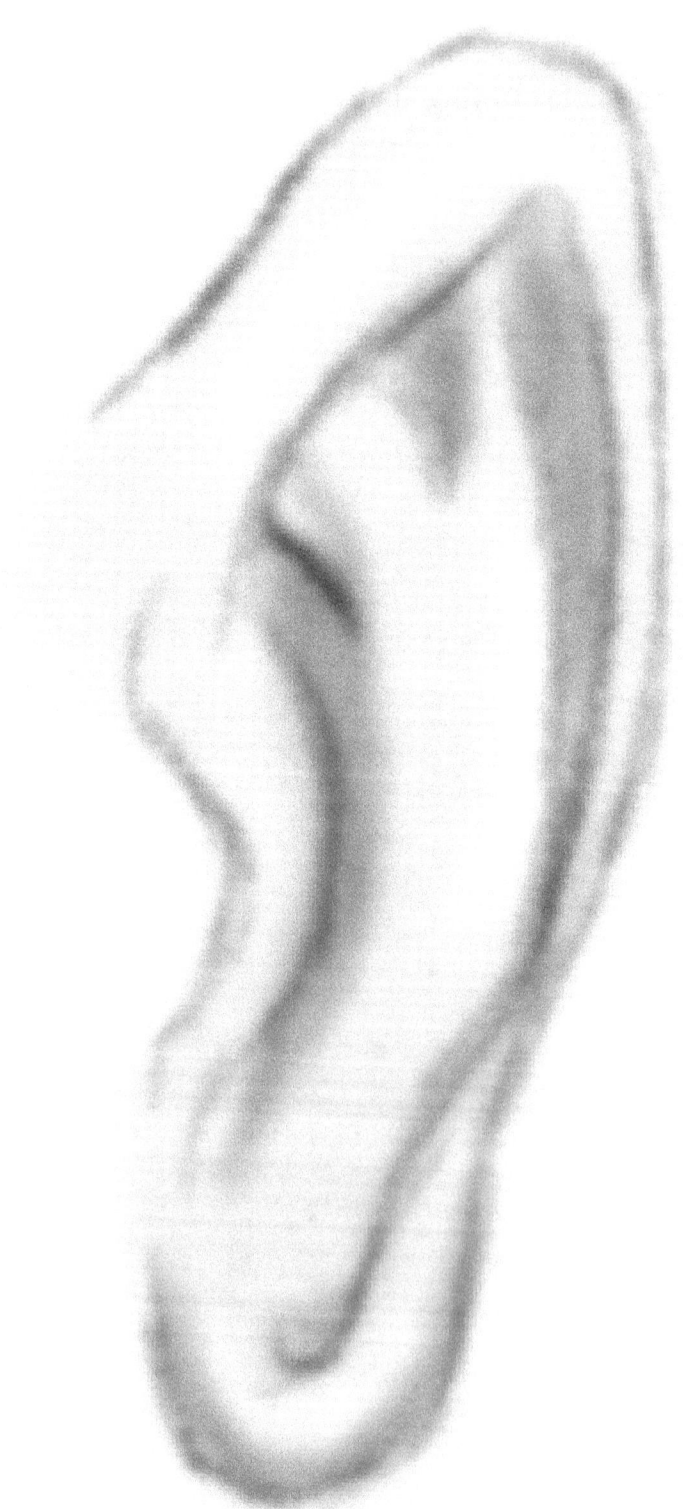

How to draw the Lips

Step 1

Drawing the lips we start off pretty much the same as the eyes. We draw the rough outline.

Step 2

Shade the upper and lower lips. For better effect, draw lines from where the lips meet going outward following their shape.

Step 3

Start adding the shadows to give it some depth.

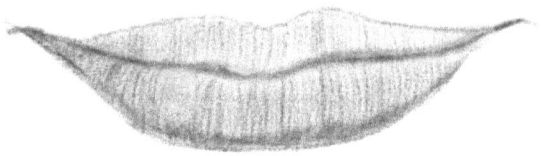

Step 4

Add some fine details, darken the edges and add some highlights

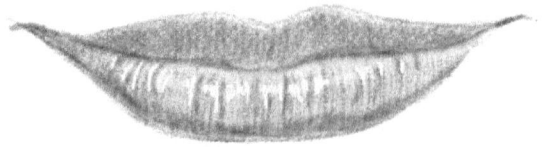

Step 5

Finalize your artwork with some toning.

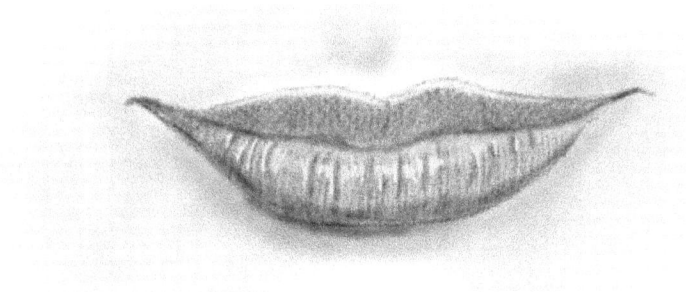

How to draw the Hair

Step 1

Again we star with a rough outline but include some details for this one.

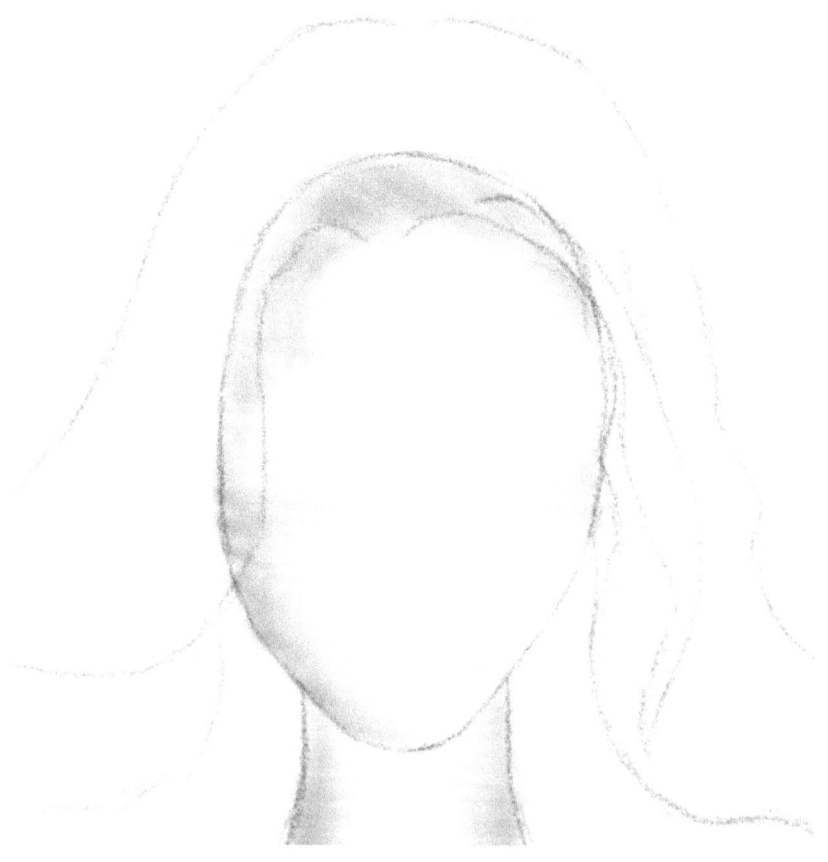

Step 2

Start doing the strands, starting from the top front, working your way back then down. Try using long strokes to simulate real.

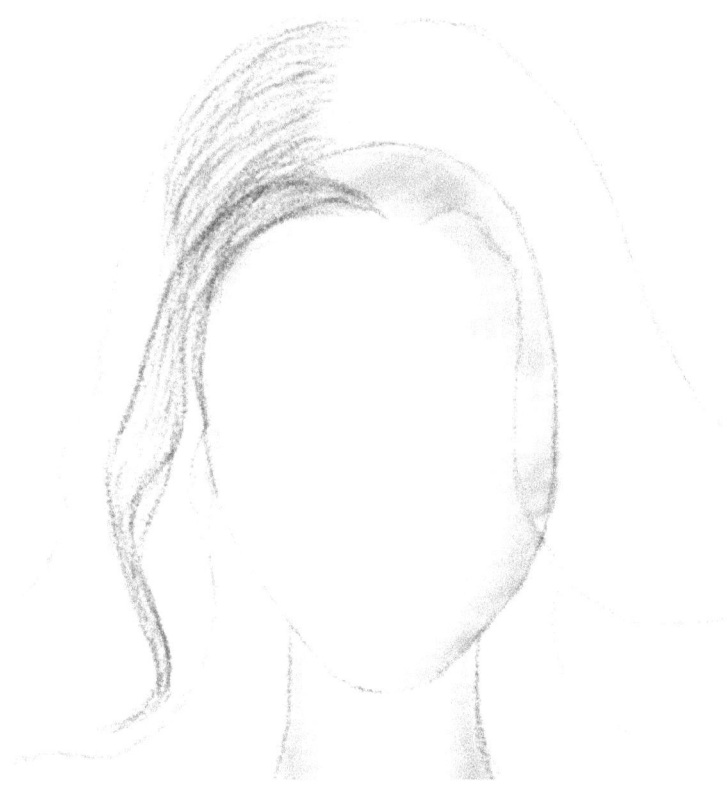

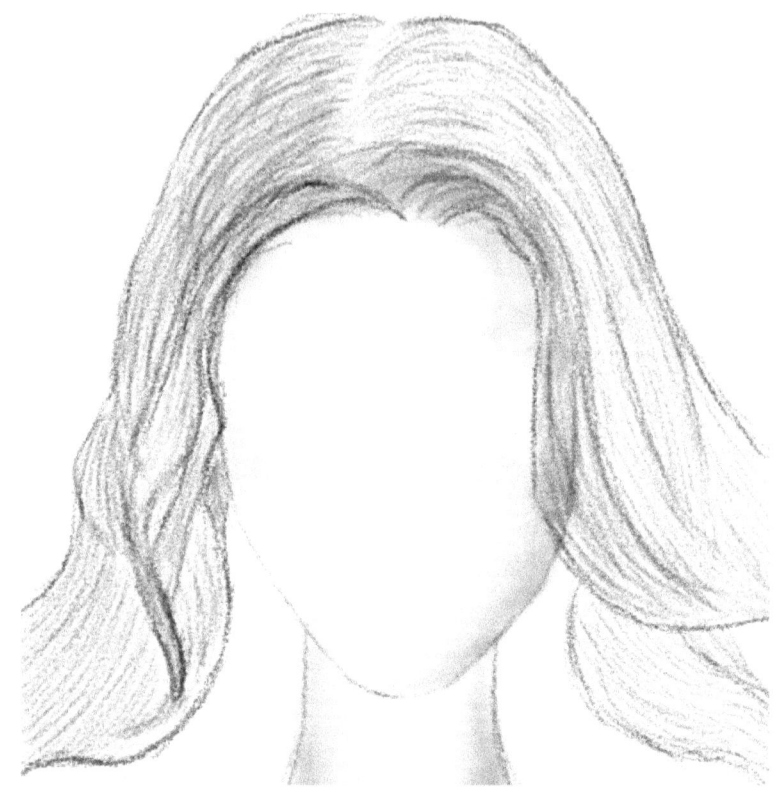

Step 3

When you've completed the strands and you're satisfied, use an eraser to highlight the parts of the hair that you think will be shiny.

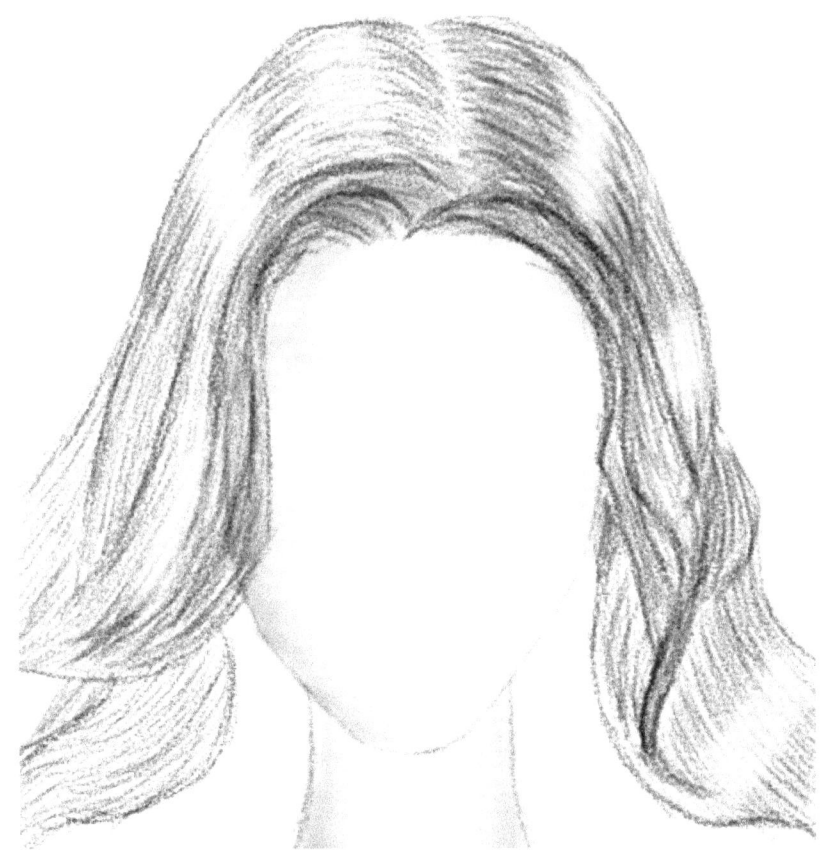

Step 4

Once you're satisfied doing the highlights, you can add the shadows, no need to smudge for the shadows, just apply a lot of lines that follow the flow of the hair.

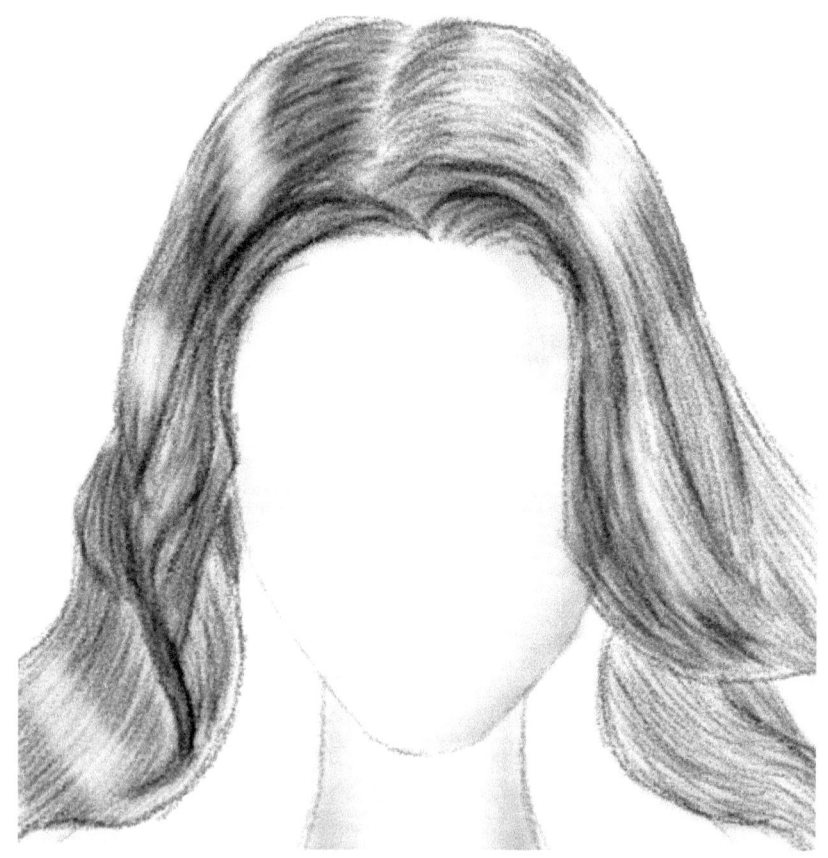

Step 5

Add some finishing touches and don't forget about the part of the hair that is behind the head or else your portrait will look like it's missing a lot of hair.

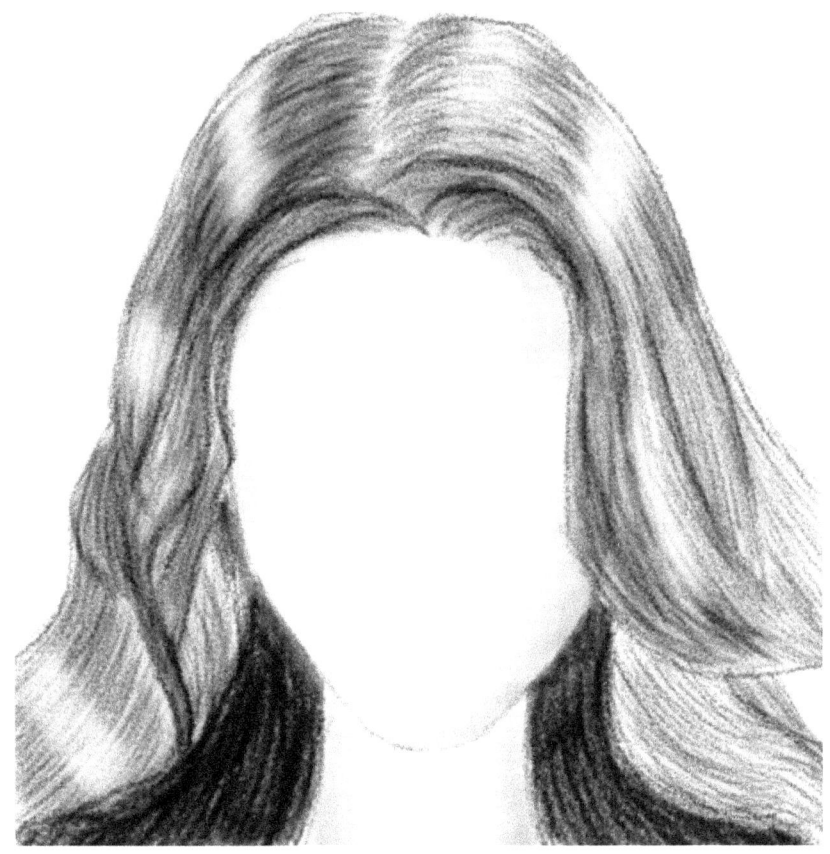

Outline and proportions

After choosing a model, you can now do the outlines of your portrait. Use the light outline technique to create the guidelines. The ruler will come in handy with the measurements to make sure the proportions of the face is correct. The eyes are usually the key point of the portrait. You can either do this freehand or by using the grid method, however, you have to have a lot of practice before going freehand.

The Devil is in the details

If you can't fill out the details from top to bottom, it is best to use a spare sheet of paper or tissue paper under your hand to act as a shield and minimize smudging. After filling out the features of the face, add as many details as you can. Don't rush making it detailed, because those small details will be the ones to make it stand out from the work of others. You can even use a mechanical pencil to add details to the eyes and hair. Make sure that there is a balanced flow of darks, mid tones and lights. Double-check the proportions of your drawing against the model by looking at it upside-down or in the mirror.

Patience, practice and enjoy

Do not expect your portraits to become perfect or realistic right away. It takes great mastery and skill before you can draw freehand realistic and living portraits. So you really need to have lots of patience to practice frequently. Try to develop your own drawing style. And most importantly, don't forget to enjoy what you are doing!

Chapter 5 - Memory Drawing

This is an advanced technique that even intermediate artists have a hard time doing. But practicing this early on, and alternating it with your standard drawing, will help broaden your imagination. Soon you will find yourself capable of naturally altering subjects as you draw them. Like altering your subject's hairstyle, or moving the objects on reference. Your first attempts will probably be disappointing, but don't fret! Memory drawing is all about errors and taking note of these errors and making a point of not repeating them. Below are steps on how you can practice drawing from memory.

Step 1

For starters, choose a fairly easy subject or reference, like a vase, a plant or in my case I chose a plate of cookies and a cup of tea.

Step 2

Take a good look at your subject, you can look at it at different angles but as you are just beginning I suggest you pick an angle and concentrate on that view. Study the light source, see where the shadows fall and how dark they are. If there are multiple light sources, take note of where they are coming from and take note of how the shadows overlap each other.

Step 3

Once you've had a good look, get your sketch pad and start drawing your reference without looking at it once until you're done with your drawing. Don't stress out too much if you can't remember some aspects of it. Just draw what you can remember.

Step 4

When you're done with your drawing, compare it to your subject and take note of the errors you made, remember, as mentioned above, memory drawing is all about making errors and keeping in mind not to make those errors again.

Step 5

Now get another clean sheet of paper or a blank page on your sketchpad and start drawing your subject again. Repeat these steps until you're satisfied with the outcome.

Step 6

When you think you've finally drawn your subject properly, start another run by looking at it at a different angle or better yet, look for another subject you can practice on.

Useful tips for Memory drawing

Here are the step-by-step useful tips on how to enhance your memory by means drawing.

Clearly scan the image or object

Study every single angle and detail of the image or object you wish to draw. Remember that you will completely rely in your sharp memory to use this technique.

Try to sketch the outline little by little

Take away the image or object out of your sight and try to draw it little by little by envisioning it inside your mind.

Begin the drawing from the easiest outlines by using the shapes as your guide. Once you're done with the major details, continue drawing the intricate details from memory.

Add further details for finishing touches

Little by little, add the details to finalize your drawings.

Take a glance on the image or object whenever

Whenever you forget some outlines of the object/image you wish to draw, take a glance of it, take the image or object away and continue drawing. This is not a cheating action; it is an act of practicing the technique.

Darken the specific areas and details

Once you're done with the object's outline, darken some areas and outlines to bring dimension on your drawing.

Draw the same image or object many times

Place the image or object in front of you and draw it many times until you familiarize every detail and outline.

Draw the details from your memory

If you feel like familiarizing the image or object by using the Memory drawing technique, draw it several times.

Compare the object or image from your Memory drawing

Get your reference object or take a look at the original image and compare it to your Memory drawing. If it needs further enhancements, don't hesitate to keep on practicing.

Draw it again looking at the original image or object

Practice by drawing it all over again with the original image or object place in front of you.

Start a new paper and draw it from memory again

Then again, start a new paper and use Memory drawing again. Do this as many times as you can until your mind and system familiarize this kind of technique.

Chapter 6 - Drawings From Imagination

Some people (some of them will even be artists themselves but mostly they just be critics) will tell you that drawing from your imagination is the hardest thing to do and there is no way to properly teach it. For a part they are true, there is no formal way of teaching someone to draw what is in their mind, as only they can see it, it is in their mind after all. But there are ways of teaching you how to train yourself, to train your brain and your hand coordination to properly draw images in your mind. Once you get the hang of it, this will be your greatest ally when it comes to drawing. You'll be able to create things that, before, only existed in your imagination. You can now share things that only you used to be able to see.

To be able to do this, as in all things related to art, you need to practice. One good way to achieve this is by following the previous chapter on drawing from memory. This is pretty much the same concept, except for the slight difference of the source of your reference. Instead of it being a real subject, it will mostly come from just your mind. I say "mostly" because at some point, consciously or not, some part of your subjects design will have come from something you have seen or heard. Don't worry, there's no shame in that, you are only at the beginning of your drawing career, getting ideas from other subjects or even art works cannot be helped. Just make sure you don't copy it exactly as it is, because that will just be, well, copying it, it wouldn't be coming from your imagination anymore, would it? It's ok to get ideas and altering them until you get the hang of drawing from your imagination.

Here's a quick tip that might help you achieve this goal:

Remember the image

When you draw from imagination, you are actually producing what image you saw in your mind. You need to remember the details like, "what image it was?", "what's the colour?" And lastly, "what is the important part of the image that you need to highlight?" If for example you imagine a Unicorn you can try to look for a picture or take a photo of a horse and a horn. Several available references can be used such as books, magazines or the internet. Put these pictures together to come up with a clear image of a Unicorn then voila! You already have the image you are thinking of. All you need is to put your personal touch with a bit more flair and different style that completely represents you in that drawing.

Draw like a Pro

Superheroes are some of the common images that we imagine most of the time. You might ask yourself "how do I start drawing something I haven't seen"? It might be easy for some but for those who are just starting, they need to be more creative. You can start by making a line for your chosen figure. It depends on what action you picture them to be: standing, running, walking or sitting. Add the other important details like arms, neck, chest, limbs and so on. Make use of shapes to distinguish the body part. You can use circles for the face, oval for the palms, shoulders and feet, rectangle for the body and diagonal or the legs. Then with the use of a thicker coloured pen, make a more defined feature of the face, upper limbs, lower limbs and the entire body. Make it as close to the shape you create as this acts as your pattern. Next, you can put some pertinent details to the costume like mask, boots, belt and other stuff. Lastly, you now need to color the image depending on your preference.

If you want it to be as close as possible on how you see it in your mind, try to recollect all the details that you could possibly remember. For example if you are imagine an image of a monster then continue building it by drawing them step by step, little by little until you've completed the image. Once the image is already there, enhance the image and add more life in the image that you've produced.

As you go along your practice, make sure you use the techniques taught on previous chapters, if you're drawing a portrait, make sure you use the oval and four guidelines to properly portray your subject. To give it variety, use the different hand positions shown in chapter 2 and to give it realism and depth, use the toning techniques you've learned in chapter 3. These techniques aren't only used for drawing real life subjects they can be used in any kind of drawings, especially drawings from your imagination.

Here are few steps to get your juices going:

When drawing from your imagination, it a good practice to jot down details of your subject or in this case the character I'm creating. For this example, we will be creating an exo-suited female warrior wielding the powers of fire. You can even create a back story for your character to help you better draw them. For example:

The character we will be creating was curse as a child. The curse forces a non-lethal spontaneous combustion upon her so in order to contain the flame bursting from her body, a suit of armor was built for her. In time she learned how to control some of the flame to the extent the she was capable of flight.

Now that we have established details of our character, we can start drawing her. We will not delve too much in deep details for this character but we highly recommend that you do when creating your own character.

Step 1

Using a few shapes, like circles and rectangles, you can create a dummy marionette to help you set your character's pose. Don't worry about it not being accurate enough, this will just be your guide, and make sure not to draw to darkly, just dark enough to help you see it but light enough as to not ruin your drawing.

Step 2

When you've set your character's pose, start drawing a rough outline of their body.

Step 3

Using the outline of the body as guide, start adding the details of your character. Again don't worry about making it perfect just yet.

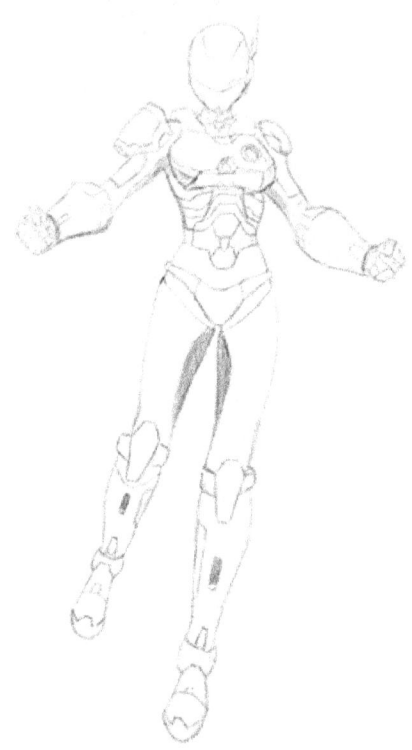

Step 4

When you're satisfied with how your character looks, you can now finalize the details, and strengthen the lines of your drawing and erase all unnecessary lines.

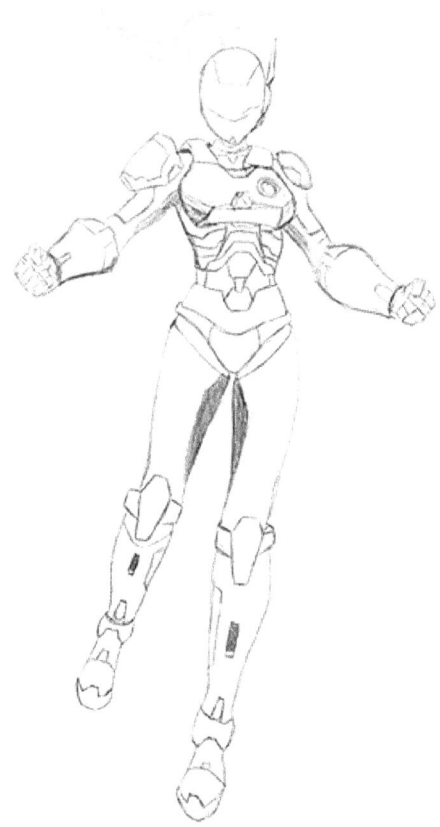

Step 5

Now add a little more detail by toning.

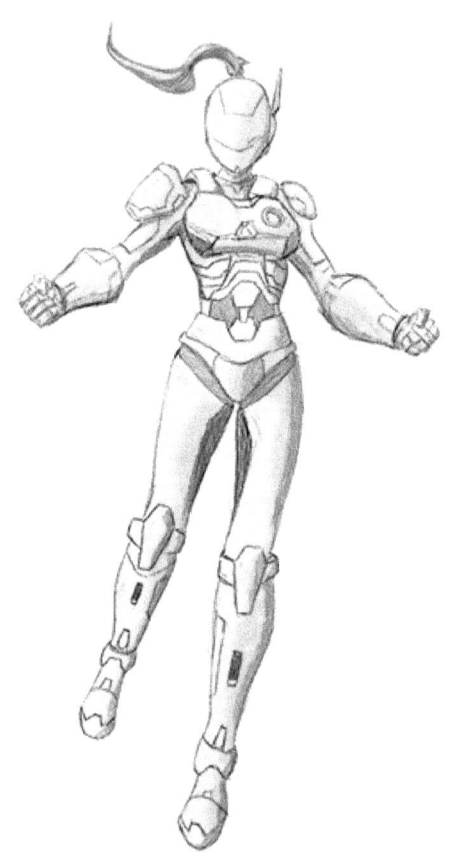

Step 6

Add the finishing touches like effects or small details

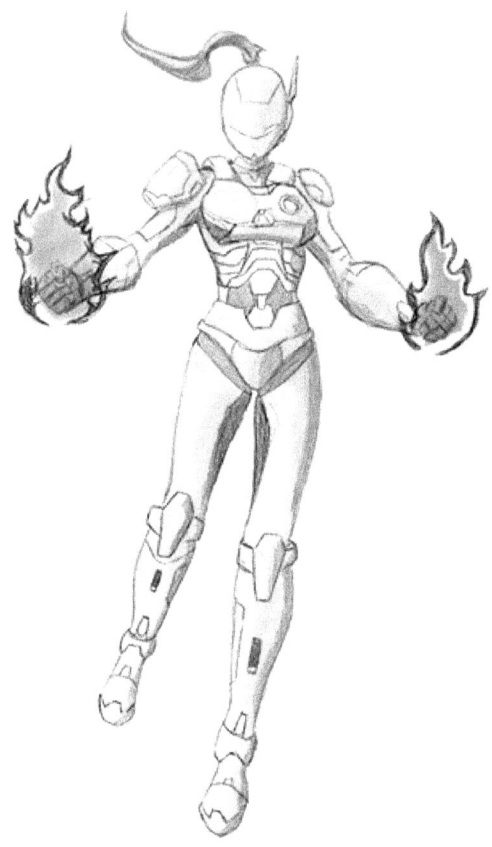

Chapter 7 - Common Drawing Mistakes

Here are some of the common mistakes when you are starting to draw:

Sticking to one subject

As a beginner, it is understandable that you would like to draw something that you love or can relate to. Than is just fine, at first at least, but make sure you try out other subject matters too. Like if you love cars and started to learn drawing from drawing cars, once you think you've perfected it, don't be afraid to venture to other subjects like portraits or landscapes. There is no problem with being good at one subject but the best thing for your drawing career is to expand to other subjects as well. For example: if you are good at drawing cars, why not try doing landscapes next, this way, you can add backgrounds and foregrounds to your car drawings.

Proportions

Some artists tend to overlook this part. Like when drawing a human figure, some mostly concentrate on the face and perfecting it first before proceeding with the other parts of the body. This will most often than not leave them with very little space for the rest of the body. This is why some drawings seem to have bubble heads. When you start your drawing, make sure your keep in mind the whole concept. Consider the space that it will occupy to be able to portray the whole concept. Cropping is part of drawing artistry, but there are proper ways of cropping your subject, in human figures for example, only crop the body at the waste, knees and ankles this will give you proper composition of your subject.

Heavy Guidelines

Guidelines are meant to be, well, guidelines. They should not appear on your final product. So make sure to make them just dark enough to be seen by you and light enough that it will not hinder the final outcome of your drawing. Try using hard pencils and using a very light lines.

Not Having a Goal

Before your start your drawing set a goal. And make sure as you go along, that you have your target in sight, don't deviate, not too much at least. Some alterations from your original goal may be good for the final product.

Detailing too early

It is very tempting to add details to your drawing early on in the process. But make sure you lay out all the necessary parts of your drawing first. Lay out the base of your drawing first. Start with the larger parts of the drawing and work your way into the smaller, finer details.

Fear of mistakes

Not all mistakes are bad, some may even be good for your drawing. But most mistakes will help you be better at drawing. Learn from them, every time you think you made a mistake, study it, and make sure you find a way to work around it, never do it again or even use it as an improvement to your drawing. I know this is cliché but everybody makes mistakes, and everybody knows this, its accepting it which is the hard part.

Knowing enough

One thing you have to keep in your mind as you start learning how to draw is that you will never know enough, you will always learn something new as long as your mind is open to improvements. If you keep an open mind, you will always find a new technique to use when drawing, a new concept you can apply or a new way of lay outing.

Create your own style

This is something that I can definitely not teach you, this is one thing your will have to discover by yourself, and most often than not, this is something you will develop unconsciously. Eventually as you keep on drawing, you will have your own style, it may be in the way you lay down your strokes or how you apply your shadows or simply the way your draw your lines. Just let it happen, don't think too much about it, it will eventually show.

Conclusion

Learning how to draw is a wonderful and very useful skill especially if you've mastered such craft. Imagine the wonderful possibilities of being able to draw beautiful creations, different places – it's like telling a story. Heck, one day you might even belong to one of those artists that draw famous cartoons like Frozen or famous comic strips like the Avengers or Justice League.

In the early years people used drawing to communicate when there were no words yet. It has always been a part of their life. Today, knowing the basics in drawing is essential in creating these works of art but of course as you move on, you will be able to master them and create more vivid and unique pieces. Not only does it make you express yourself but you can also make use of it to earn as well.

So now that you have read the whole book, it's your turn! Go ahead, apply and share what you have learned. Be creative and express yourself. I hope I have already given you useful tips and the knowledge to create beautiful, wonderful drawings – and most of all grow and continue to improve. Don't worry if at first you might have some difficulties, it's natural. Always keep in mind that practice makes perfect. The only way that you will be able to perfect this art is to – DRAW, DRAW, DRAW.

Lastly, if you enjoyed this book, then I'd like to ask you for a favor, would you be kind enough to leave a review for this book on Amazon? It'd be greatly appreciated! Again, thank you very much.

Follow and pursue your dream! Start drawing your work of art.

If you enjoyed the information in this book, please go to your online eBook provider and leave a positive review. It would be greatly appreciated.

Thank you for reading!

Dear Reader,

I would like to invite you to join my email list! This way you will never miss a new release, and even get new Kindle books for FREE – because we will drop you a line when they are on free promotion on Amazon!

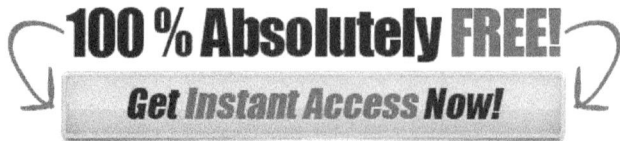

<u>Click here</u> to get instant access to all our FREE books now!

(Click the link or enter http://bit.ly/19eWRoW into your browser.)